THE BEST OF
Australian
Birds

THE BEST OF
Australian
Birds

DAVE WATTS

NEW
HOLLAND

To Helen, my partner
and best friend.

First published in Australia in 1999 by
New Holland Publishers (Australia) Pty Ltd
Sydney • Auckland • London • Cape Town

14 Aquatic Drive Frenchs Forest NSW 2086 Australia
218 Lake Road Northcote Auckland
24 Nutford Place London W1H 6DQ United Kingdom
80 McKenzie Street Cape Town 8001 South Africa

National Library of Australia Cataloguing-in-Publication Data:

Watts, Dave
The best of Australian birds

ISBN 1 86436 461 0.

1.Birds—Australia. I. Title.

598.0994

Publishing General Manager: Jane Hazell
Publisher: Averill Chase
Editor: Howard Gelman
Designer: Susanne Geppert
Reproduction: Colour Symphony
Printer: Bangunan Times Publishing

Half title page: Princess Parrot
Opposite title page: Kookaburra
Title page: Australasian Gannet
Acknowledgements page: Red-tailed Black Cockatoo

Contents

Acknowledgements

Over the course of obtaining photographs for this book, I have received help from a great many people. In particular, I wish to thank the various officers and rangers of National Parks and Wildlife Services across Australia. In Tasmania: Peter Brown, Nick Mooney, Mark Holdsworth, Sally Bryant, Ray Brereton, Robbie Gaffney, Cathie Plowman, Daryl Binns, Ian Marmion, Jans and Katina Howe, David Montgomery, Gary Sutton and Brian Carson. My sincere thanks also to the various officers in the field in Victoria, South Australia, Queensland and the Northern Territory.

I received a great deal of help at the Desert Park, Alice Springs. A special thanks to Ian Cawood, Paul Mander and Rodney Hare. The staff at 'Birds Australia' have been supremely helpful at all times and so gracious in publishing some of my pictures. My sincere thanks to David Baker-Gabb, Kate Fitzherbert, Merrilyn Julian and Lee O'Mahoney. Chris Hassell and Jan Sparrow, wardens at Broome Bird Observatory were so supportive and inspiring. Their assistance in guiding me to prime bird locations is greatly appreciated.

Dirk Hartog Island is a very special place. Many thanks to Kieran and Tory for allowing me to photograph some of the wonderful birds which are found there. I owe a debt also to Jim Milne of Nullarbor Roadhouse, Nobby Clark from Mary River Houseboats and David Croft and Lisa Silva at Fowler's Gap Research Station.

It is always a pleasure to work with the staff at New Holland Publishers. I would especially like to thank Averill Chase, Jane Hazell, Howard Gelman, Susanne Geppert and Raquel Hill for their help and support with this project.

My greatest and most sincere thanks go to Helen Sargeant, my partner, for being so tolerant of my long working hours and for being so loving and supportive of my work.

Introduction

The heat was almost unbearable as I waited in my small hide overlooking a gnarled and fire-ravaged native pine tree in the Mallee region of north-west Victoria. A quivering screech alerted me and suddenly a Major Mitchell's Cockatoo landed on a branch in a flurry of pink and white. With a comical bobbing of the head, one of the world's most beautiful parrots strutted before me, its yellow and scarlet crest raised in defiance. Before the cockatoo clambered head-first into the tree hollow to feed its three awaiting chicks, I had finished half a roll of film.

I was elated, but I would have to wait several weeks until returning home before viewing the results. Only then would I know whether the effort resulted in success or failure. At least I still had the memory of those enchanting moments spent so close to one of Australia's most beautiful birds.

As long as I can remember, I have been passionately interested in nature, especially birds. During my early years in the wilds of south Devon, England, I had ample opportunity to indulge this passion, frequently to the consternation of my parents.

I vividly remember seeing from my bedroom window the most exotic bird imaginable feeding among a group of Common Starlings. It was a scarlet and grey bird with a crimson crest, and I could not discover a bird remotely similar in my field guide. After an inquiry to the local museum the verdict was a Crimson-crested Cardinal, probably an escapee from a nearby aviary.

Was it really possible that an overwhelming variety of brilliantly coloured and exotic birds lived out their lives on faraway continents? And so the desire to travel led me eventually to Australia, frequently known as *Terra Psittacorum*—the Land of Parrots.

We will probably never know just how many species of birds have existed within Australia since they first evolved from their reptilian ancestors during the late Jurassic period over 140 million years ago. We do know that out of a total of approximately 9000 species living worldwide at present, Australia is fortunate to be home to around 750 species. Incredibly, 60 per cent of these are endemic and about 130 are regular visitors which do not breed within Australia. Due to the vast areas of hostile environment it is only recently that great gains have been made in the area of avifaunal research. Because of the rapid progress in this research, it is now recognised that many species of Australian birds are highly nomadic or semi-nomadic due to the vagaries of climate and the frequency of drought.

Australia is home to many of the groups of birds that are found elsewhere on our planet—raptors, kingfishers, ducks, flycatchers and crows. Many of the dominant bird groups though, such as the bowerbirds, honeyeaters, fairy-wrens, currawongs and the nocturnal frogmouths, are quite unique to Australia or are found in few other parts of the world. Although parrots and cockatoos do occur on most continents, only in Australia have they evolved into such a bewildering and spectacular display of colour and form.

The earliest known feathered animal which was capable of a gliding flight at least is the somewhat reptilian and famous *Archaeopteryx lithographica*, the most primitive known ancestor of modern day birds. The complete fossilised remains were discovered in a German quarry where they had lain for approximately 140 million years. From Victoria comes the earliest known evidence of any Australian bird, in the form of a few feathers which have been dated to 110 million years ago.

The fact that Australia broke away and drifted from other land masses during the break-up of Gondwana helps explain why several major bird groups such as

A quivering screech alerted me and suddenly a Major Mitchell's Cockatoo landed on a branch in a flurry of pink and white.

sandgrouse, vultures, pheasants, woodpeckers and barbets are not represented here. These birds evolved elsewhere after Australia had broken away.

The discovery of fossil bones in the Lake Eyre region has demonstrated that flamingos lived in central Australia over 5 million years ago. During this period much of inland Australia was still covered by rainforest, large lake systems and several slow-flowing rivers.

That the origins of Australian avifauna can be traced back to the break-up of the super-continent Gondwana can be seen in the similarities between certain Australian species and some species which still exist in South America and Africa. The large flightless ratites—Emu, Cassowary, Ostrich and Rhea—have all originated from an early ancestor from Gondwana. It is clear that these birds have been flightless for many millions of years as they all lack a deep keel on the breastbone for the attachment of flight muscles. The other extinct ratites include the giant Moas from New Zealand, some of which grew to over 4 metres tall, and the Elephant Birds from Madagascar.

One of the most distinctive of all birds, the big and colourful Southern Cassowary, is a highly specialised ratite found in the forests of north Queensland where it is endangered. This potent symbol of tropical rainforests is shy and rarely seen. Being a frugivor (fruit eater) the Southern Cassowary is sometimes attracted to orchards or gardens where it may become tame.

The most striking feature of the Southern Cassowary is the horned head or casque which consists of a core of cartilage covered by a hardened skin. The casque helps to protect the Southern Cassowary's head as the bird moves rapidly through the rainforest. Females are usually larger than males and have taller casques and more colourful wattles. Unfortunately the endangered Southern Cassowary is threatened by destruction of its rainforest habitat, particularly on the lowland plains where approximately 60 per cent of available habitat has been cleared, mainly for sugarcane farms.

Australia's other ratite, the Emu, is a familiar and widespread bird which is our national bird emblem.

Species of smaller emu once occurred on Tasmania, King Island and Kangaroo Island but were wiped out by settlers last century. These emus hold the dubious record of being the only species of birds known to have become definitely extinct in recent years within Australia.

The omnivorous Emu is a nomadic wanderer which may be encountered almost anywhere on the Australian mainland, although it prefers open woodland, scrub and plains, avoiding dense forest. The Emu is superbly adapted to its often hostile environment. Being omnivorous, Emus are able to take advantage of prevailing conditions and their diet consists of flowers and seeds of small shrubs, young sprouting grasses and insects, particularly during grasshopper plagues.

Perhaps less familiar are the myriad seabirds to be found around Australia's incredibly rich and varied coastline which extends over 36,000 kilometres. One of the joys of living in Australia is being able to visit and explore some of the countless islands which are strung like a handful of pearls around the Australian coast.

The male Emu incubates 6 to 12 eggs and continues parental care for up to 18 months.

Huge numbers of Sooty Terns nest on some offshore islands including Lord Howe and Houtman Albrolhos.

Australasian Gannets recently established Australia's only mainland colony at Cape Portland, Victoria.

Of particular importance are the coral cays of the Great Barrier Reef which provide ideal breeding conditions for millions of Wedge-tailed Shearwaters, Great and Least Frigatebirds, Red-tailed Tropicbirds and several species of tern. During the breeding season open areas of these islands are frequently packed with dense colonies consisting of many thousands of seabirds such as Crested Terns, Bridled Terns and Sooty Terns, while Pisonia and Casuarina trees are alive with nesting Black Noddies.

Many islands of the Great Barrier Reef, such as Michaelmas Cay and Lady Elliot Island, are promoted as suitable for ecotourism. Effective controls and management of tourists are avoiding disturbance to breeding birds while allowing birdwatchers and photographers to experience nature at close quarters. These romantic coral cays are among the world's finest locations for photographing seabirds and other wildlife.

Islands in Bass Strait provide important refuges for some of the larger species of seabirds such as Australasian Gannets which breed in densely packed colonies on Black Pyramid and Lawrence Rocks near Portland, Victoria. The Shy Albatross also has major breeding colonies on Albatross Island in Bass Strait and The Mewstone off southwest Tasmania. Bass Strait is also a stronghold for Little Penguins which occur right around the coast of southern Australia. The world's smallest penguin is unusual in being nocturnal on land, coming ashore only after dark.

Flocks of Australian Pelicans are a feature of coastal lagoons and beaches as well as inland wetlands around much of Australia. Although somewhat comical and clumsy on land, pelicans are magnificent in flight, soaring effortlessly to great heights, sometimes in large flocks. Fossil remains of pelicans discovered in Australia have been dated to between 30 and 40 million years ago; these prehistoric pelicans are very similar to the present day species. Flocks of Australian Pelicans often fish together by swimming slowly in formation and driving fish into the shallows, then scooping them up with their huge bills.

Eagles, hawks, harriers, kites and falcons are all here, integral features of the Australian landscape enriching many a visitor's journey into the outback. Birds of prey are well represented within Australia with a total of 24 species occurring on a regular basis. Several of these species are endemic to Australia, including the large and spectacular Wedge-tailed Eagle, Square-tailed Kite, Black-breasted Buzzard, Red Goshawk, Black Falcon, Grey Falcon and Nankeen Kestrel.

The attitude of human beings towards raptors has been ambivalent. On the one hand we admire their skill as hunters with superb powers of flight and extraordinary eyesight and yet we ruthlessly persecute many species, such as the magnificent Wedge-tailed Eagle, for purportedly killing lambs and other domesticated animals. Fortunately public opinion has now swung towards conservation of these spectacular birds and there are many areas within Australia where birds of prey are easily watched and even photographed.

Since being protected, Wedge-tailed Eagles have recovered their numbers and are now frequently seen perched on dead trees beside outback roads or feeding on road-killed kangaroos. There are some excellent areas in the country for viewing Wedgies (as they are affectionately known) particularly the Silver City Highway north of Broken Hill to Tibooburra and Sturt

The largest Australian raptor is the Wedge-tailed Eagle which has a wingspan up to two metres. The diet consists largely of mammals (especially rabbits), carrion and reptiles.

National Park, and the Stuart Highway between Coober Pedy and north to the border of the Northern Territory.

The tree-lined streets, parks, gardens and lakes of Canberra are particularly attractive to raptors, and several species nest within the city limits. A visitor to the city may, with luck, see Little Eagle, White-bellied Sea-Eagle, Brown Goshawk, Whistling Kite, Black-shouldered Kite, Brown Falcon and Nankeen Kestrel all on the same day.

Several of Australia's raptors such as Red Goshawk or Grey Falcon are rarities eagerly sought by enthusiastic birdwatchers. The Red Goshawk is an enigmatic bird which is limited to the coastal woodlands and gorges of northern and northeastern Australia. Visitors to Kakadu National Park should look out for this large goshawk particularly over tree-lined rivers and gorges where it preys on lorikeets and other small birds and mammals. The slender-winged and beautiful Grey Falcon is similar to a Peregrine Falcon in flight and is widespread, although rarely seen, across the arid areas of central and northwestern Australia.

Some of the most visible and colourful birds are the many and varied species of parrot (approximately 60) which are found in virtually every part of the landscape. People living in the humid forest areas of eastern Australia are likely to notice several species visiting their gardens, including Australian King Parrots, Crimson Rosellas and Sulphur-crested Cockatoos.

Some species such as the nomadic and familiar Budgerigar and the Galah are widespread across much of the mainland. Other species, such as the Orange-bellied Parrot, Palm Cockatoo and Red-capped Parrot, can be seen only in very restricted ranges.

The dominant and largest group of Australian parrots are the rosellas, related ringnecks and grass parrots or *neophemas*. These small to medium parrots are almost exclusively Australian and are found throughout the mainland and Tasmania. Most are generalised feeders and these include the Ground Parrot, the Eastern Rosella, the Red-rumped Parrot, the Rock Parrot and Mallee Ringneck.

One of the finest areas to view parrots in the wild is the Mallee area of south central Australia which is home to a large number of species. Mallee Ringnecks, Purple-crowned Lorikeets and Galahs squabble over hollows in ancient mallee trees while Major Mitchell's Cockatoos prefer the jagged hollows of native pines and are frequently seen feeding on wild melons along the roadsides.

One rare member of the parrot family is the Orange-bellied Parrot. Today, they number fewer than 200 individuals and they breed only in Tasmania's southwest wilderness. They nest in tree hollows in patches of rainforest overlooking vast Button-grass plains and feed on the small flowers and seeds of low-growing herbs. In autumn, they migrate, via King Island, to the mainland and spend the winter feeding among saltmarsh vegetation and other low plants mainly in coastal areas of the southeast.

Some of the most popular and distinctive parrots are the cockatoos, of which several species occur in most regions of Australia. The well-known Cockatiel is generally regarded as having a close affinity to the cockatoos due to the fine tapering crest and the lack of pigment

Budgerigars are particularly vocal and quite easy to approach during courtship.

Flocks of extremely noisy and raucous Sulphur-crested Cockatoos are a common sight in eastern Australia. Both parents incubate the eggs for the 1 to 3 chicks.

which gives other parrots their green appearance. Flocks of up to several hundred Cockatiels are regularly encountered across much of inland Australia where they are found perched in large dead trees.

Among the most interesting are the large, noisy and conspicuous black cockatoos. The Yellow-tailed Black Cockatoo remains common in many areas of southwest and southeastern Australia including Tasmania where they may be seen in a variety of habitats from sea level to the subalpine areas.

The Red-tailed Black Cockatoo is the most widely distributed of all the black cockatoos and a common bird across much of northern and western Australia. The most striking feature of the male is a brilliant band of vermilion across the tail. Flocks of over 100 individuals of these birds are an impressive sight as they float buoyantly over the treetops, calling to one another with a rolling, metallic 'kree' or 'kerr-uur'.

Some of the finest places to watch or to photograph birds in Australia are the many dams or waterholes scattered across the continent particularly those in the arid zone. I well remember waiting beside a rapidly shrinking waterhole last November in the far northwest of New South Wales. I was up well before sunrise in order to be

During the breeding season, the endangered Orange-bellied Parrot may be watched from a public hide at Melaleuca, Tasmania.

in place before the sky began to brighten. I hid under a small bush with a sheet of camouflage netting thrown over myself and my tripod and camera. It had been a particularly dry spring that year, partly due to the El Niño effect, which meant the gibber plains were dry and parched but, most importantly, the wildlife in this area desperately needed to drink.

Already a male Emu and six rapidly growing striped chicks are making their way towards the far end of the waterhole. Suddenly a Wedge-tailed Eagle glides slowly into view, flying low it swoops towards the Emu chicks which scatter in alarm. The Wedge-tailed Eagle misses and lands in a dead tree to await the rising sun to warm the air which will improve its powers of flight.

A familiar warbling alerts me and a small flock of about 150 Budgerigars arrive with swift and erratic flight and settle close by the water's edge. A few birds scramble along a dead branch and drink quickly before the flock departs suddenly, spooked by some unseen fear. I hadn't moved. I was perfectly still but perhaps they sensed something out of place. By now the rapidly rising sun is warming the cool morning air as a family of Black-tailed Native Hens runs across the open ground to drink. I notice a movement in the distance and, slowly lifting my binoculars see an Australian Pratincole and then a second nearby. They run elegantly, stopping now and then to bob up and down before running again to snatch an insect from the bare ground. I hadn't noticed them arrive—perhaps they were there all along.

With much screeching a flock of about 50 Galahs arrives and the birds perch in the topmost branches of a dead tree, their pink and white plumage in contrast to the deep blue sky. All around is activity—the sparkling flashes of Crimson Chats, a gaudy troop of Cockatiels, the comical squabbling and posturing of a large party of Apostlebirds and the scurrying between bushes of a pair of Cinnamon Quail-thrushes, their rufous backs gleaming in the early morning sun.

Many of Australia's birds are nomadic seed eaters. They include the beautiful grass-finches of which approximately 18 species can be found in Australia, mainly within the tropics. Most grass-finches are highly social birds frequently gathering in small to large flocks with some species nesting in loose colonies. Australian grass-finches are all monogamous and the males of the species perform an elaborate mating ritual which involves bobbing up and down on a perch while holding a long grass stem.

One of the best areas to see grass-finches, including the Gouldian Finch, Long-tailed Finch, Masked Finch, Star Finch, Double-barred and Zebra Finch, is the Kimberley region of northern Australia.

Among the most unusual and bizarre of all birds are the frogmouths which occur only in Australia and Papua New Guinea. Three species are found in Australia although only the Tawny Frogmouth is common and widespread. The other two species, the Marbled Frogmouth and Papuan Frogmouth, have small limited distributions in north Queensland.

The Tawny Frogmouth, frequently called a 'Mopoke', resembles an owl although it is more closely related to nightjars. These nocturnal hunters of large insects roost on branches during the day when their dappled plumage and habit of freezing allows them to go unnoticed. In fact roosting birds are wonderfully camouflaged to resemble jagged stumps of wood.

Among the most spectacular of all Australia's avian icons are the lyrebirds, named for the resemblance of the outer tail feathers of the Superb Lyrebird to a Greek lyre. Two species occur within Australia: Albert's Lyrebird which is restricted to the dense rainforests and scrub of far northwestern New South Wales and south-east Queensland; and the Superb Lyrebird which frequents the rainforests and fern gullies of the coastal south-east Australian mainland and Tasmania, where it has been introduced.

The Superb Lyrebird is the largest of all songbirds and has one of the most charismatic, rich and mellow songs of any bird. Males display during autumn and winter on earthen mounds or on nearby perches. The long filamentous tail plumes are thrown forward over the head, fanlike, while the bird prances and pours

forth a stream of song which includes much mimicry. Male Superb Lyrebirds are capable of mimicking almost any sound from water dripping or chainsaws to most other local songbirds. I heard one male Lyrebird imitating perfectly the sound of a camera shutter plus motordrive! In southern Tasmania, commonly heard bird imitations are of Yellow-tailed Black Cockatoos, as well as Yellow-throated Honeyeaters, Black and Grey Currawongs and Grey Shrike-Thrushes.

A familiar and delightful sight throughout Australia are the small family parties of fairy wrens consisting of small numbers of brightly coloured males plus a majority of brown coloured females and young males. The Superb Fairy-wren is one of the most popular birds of the south-east Australian mainland and Tasmania, and groups of these highly social birds are frequently seen in gardens. The gaudily coloured males usually moult into a female-like brown eclipse plumage at the end of the breeding season. All males however, even during the eclipse plumage, have deep blue tails.

Among the most elusive of all Australian birds are the grasswrens which are larger than fairy-wrens and are distinctively marked with long white streaks. Generally

The Tawny Frogmouth roosts motionless on a tree branch during daylight and pursues its prey at night.

Male Superb Lyrebirds perform elaborate courtship displays on earthen mounds deep within the wet south-east forests.

The Superb Fairy-Wren is a highly social bird frequently seen in the woodlands and gardens of southeast Australia.

A member of a highly advanced group, the male Satin Bowerbird struts before its elaborate bower while the female watches.

confined to arid regions infrequently visited by humans, one species, the Grey Grasswren, was not discovered until 1967. Other species such as Black Grasswren and Eyrean Grasswren are eagerly sought by enthusiastic birders and photographers alike. Grasswrens are always on the move, seeking out small seeds and insects as they scurry and rush about among the rocks, spinifex and canegrass of their remote habitats. The ability to feed on insects as well as seeds allows these small-winged inhabitants of the arid regions to gain moisture and thrive in a frequently waterless and inhospitable terrain.

Among the most characteristic and widespread of all Australian birds are the honeyeaters which have evolved to take advantage of the huge diversity of nectar-bearing plants such as grevilleas, banksias, eucalypts and acacias. Their most distinctive feature is the long flexible brush-tipped tongue which is housed in a generally long and curved bill. The function of the tongue is to collect nectar from deep within tubular flowers, resulting in honeyeaters rivalling insects as pollinators of flowering plants. Many honeyeater species are nomadic showing regular seasonal movements in response

to the blossoming of native plants. The diet is also supplemented with some insects which assist in balancing the protein and nutrient requirements. Honeyeaters exhibit considerable variation in size, ranging from the Yellow Wattlebird (the largest honeyeater and endemic to Tasmania) to the brightly-coloured Scarlet Honeyeater which inhabits mangroves and coastal forests of eastern Australia.

Possibly some of the most advanced of all birds are the bowerbirds which exhibit a remarkable habit of constructing quite elaborate bowers in which displays are performed. One of the most familiar of all is the Satin Bowerbird of eastern Australia. Males build a neat avenue of thin sticks which are pushed into the ground and daubed inside with a mixture of wood pulp, charcoal and saliva. Platforms at each end of the bower are decorated with an assortment of blue or yellow objects such as feathers, flowers, plastic pens, clothes pegs or berries. Whenever a female approaches or enters the bower, the male begins to prance, trance-like, while holding an object in his bill and uttering hissing and wheezing notes.

Strangely, the largest bower of all is built by the smallest bowerbird, the Golden Bowerbird, which is restricted to high-altitude rainforests in the wet tropics of north Queensland. Bowers are frequently built on sloping hillsides and consist of two tall columns of sticks which are woven around saplings or fern stems. A horizontal display perch is incorporated between the towers and is lavishly decorated with lichen and small pale flowers. A central area of the perch remains bare due to the frequent visits of the male bowerbird. Female Golden Bowerbirds are very timid and they visit the bower only infrequently. The deep, untidy nest is usually built in the fork of a tree and in dense forest, some distance from the bower.

The mountains, forests, wetlands and vast open plains of Australia have undergone radical changes recently, particularly during the last 200 years. The original character of the landscape has been carefully preserved within the many national parks that have been

The plumage of the Malleefowl allows this large ground-dwelling bird to remain camouflaged in its open woodland and scrub habitat where it feeds on flowers, green shoots, seeds and insects.

designated. However some of these national parks and reserves are now islands of wild nature surrounded by a vast areas that have been destroyed or radically changed and many species of birds, particularly those flightless birds such as the Malleefowl, are no longer able to maintain an exchange of genes within the greater bird population.

Birds are decreasing from a multitude of threats but none is more serious than human-induced habitat destruction. Birds are utterly dependent for shelter and food on the type of environment to which each species is adapted by evolution.

Unfortunately it is usually the most specialised birds which are the first to suffer—island species, flightless species or those birds dependent upon specific foods. Most birds show little tolerance for any form of change. The only birds which are able to adapt to these conditions are those hardy or more invasive and generalised species such as the House Sparrow, European Starling, Feral Pigeon or Cattle Egret.

A fruit-eating bird from the wet tropics rainforest is unable to survive in the monoculture of sugarcane any more than a fish-eating wetland bird can survive in a sterile expanse of wheat. In prehistoric times birds were able to adapt to natural alterations of habitat and cli-

mate because the change was gradual and measured in millions of years. Today, many birds have little hope of adapting to the massive environmental modifications which are now carried out annually. Extermination is taking place and this must rank as one of the greatest ecological tragedies yet caused by the human race.

Birds are now frequently seen as natural indicators of the health of the environment and what happens to them can alert us to the less visible threats such as acid rain, pollution and the growing threat of global warming. The decline of birds of prey due to breeding failures resulting from contamination by DDT and other persistent chemicals is now well documented. Several of these pollutants have been phased out in many countries including Australia and some of these species are now showing signs of recovery. Fortunately the disastrous decrease in number of birds of prey and predatory waterbirds was less severe in Australia due to its vast expanses and the lower pressures of a smaller human population.

Birds are certainly one of the most successful of all animal groups in terms of evolutionary diversity, due mainly to their remarkable versatility. Few groups of animals have the ability to run, climb, swim, dive and fly as well as birds do.

Fortunately the conservation ethic has now gripped the imagination of the Australian community and public awareness has become a potent force in protecting our wonderful diversity of birds.

My fascination with birds has led me to almost every corner of Australia—to vast swathes of forest, romantic coral islands, the watery tapestry of great wetlands and to dusty and forbidding deserts. Each of these habitats presents a different scene with a variety of birds inhabiting them. A great many have become indelibly etched into my consciousness and I return to them again. Each visit brings new joys and new birds.

With this book I hope to encourage you to share in and to visit some of the superb natural areas which remain in Australia and to watch and enjoy the huge variety of birds to be found in them.

Fragmentation and destruction of the diverse rainforest habitat is threatening the remaining population of the Southern Cassowary.

Wetlands

Human association with wetlands and their attendant bird life has existed here in Australia for many thousands of years. Aboriginal tribespeople, over the centuries, learnt how to obtain a rich, varied and nutritious diet from these important ecosystems, including water-plants such as Lotus Lilies, the eggs of wild ducks and geese, as well as the birds themselves.

Water is fundamental to life, and the rivers, lakes and marshes of wetlands are among the most productive habitats on earth. Within Australia, permanent wetlands persist mainly in coastal regions whereas most inland wetlands are seasonal, filling after good rains and then evaporating away during the dry season.

Most typical wetland birds are totally dependent upon the existence of these important habitats. Almost all wetland birds are nomadic, flying long distances in search of water, usually at night. Long-established flyways link many of these wetlands and the long-distance waterbirds frequently carry seeds of water plants on their feet, aiding in their dispersal and spreading them into new areas.

Millions of years ago, in what is now the Lake Eyre Basin, there existed vast permanent areas of water teeming with birdlife. These areas are now largely dry but do flood erratically, attracting large breeding concentrations of Australian Pelicans, Banded Stilts, Black-tailed Native Hens and Pink-eared Ducks. Banded Stilts are the most numerous of Australia's resident waders, with breeding colonies of up to 200 000 pairs reported on some inland salt lakes.

Lakes and marshes are the most productive wetlands and many superb examples exist in Australia. Among these are the Coorong in South Australia, Moulting Lagoon in Tasmania and the Alligator Rivers region of the Northern Territory. This latter region spans almost 20 000 square kilometres and is unusual in that almost the entire catchment lies within the Kakadu World Heritage National Park.

Large flocks of a wide range of waterbirds find refuge here. During winter months as the billabongs dry out and diminish in size, large flocks of up to 100 000 Magpie Geese may be seen. Stately Brolgas, one of the largest of all cranes, trumpet loudly at dawn while the elegant Black-necked Stork strides sedately through the shallow swamps, stabbing at frogs or fish with its massive ebony bill. Flitting excitedly across the lily pads are Comb-crested Jacanas, forever snatching at aquatic insects, their incredibly long toes allowing them to seemingly walk on water—hence the popular name of Christbird or Lily trotter. The exquisite tan-coloured eggs are covered with dark brown wavy lines and squiggles and laid on a fragile floating raft of aquatic weed.

Herons and egrets are very much a feature of tropical wetlands and large mixed gatherings of them may be seen feeding on the billabongs as they dry out. These mixed flocks are frequently composed of Pied Herons, White-necked Herons, Great and Intermediate Egrets and Royal Spoonbills.

The rich assemblage of waterbirds in turn attracts several species of raptor including the Black Kite and Whistling Kite which rarely nests far from water.

The maze of billabongs and rivers of Kakadu and the adjacent Mary River region provide perfect habitats and feeding opportunities for the magnificent White-bellied Sea-Eagle. These large and powerful eagles spend much of the day sitting on a prominent perch above the water or sometimes sailing high above on distinctive upswept wings. The massive nests are built in large trees not far from the water and are added to each year.

It is vital that the ecological quality and extent of the remaining wetlands is preserved for the conservation of these unique waterbirds.

ABOVE: *Brolgas are well known for courtship dancing.*
OPPOSITE: *A Comb-crested Jacana or Lily trotter.*

Great Egret *(Ardea alba),* ABOVE
With an almost worldwide range, this beautiful and elegant egret
nests in colonies with other waterbirds. Its long dark legs allow it
to wade into deeper water where it is able to catch frogs, fish and
aquatic invertebrates with its spear-like bill.

Massed herons and egrets, RIGHT
Large mixed gatherings of herons and egrets are often observed
feeding in tropical wetlands such as Kakadu National Park. This
group is composed of Pied Herons *(Ardea picata)*, White-necked
Herons *(Ardea pacifica)*, Intermediate Egrets, *(Ardea intermedia)*,
and some Royal Spoonbills, *(Platalea regia)*.

Brolga *(Grus rubicundus)*, OPPOSITE
This tall stately crane maintains the permanent pair bond by performing dramatic dancing displays. A pair of Brolgas usually face each other and prance about with wings held half-open, bowing and head-shaking while trumpeting loudly.

Black-necked Stork *(Ephippiorhynchus asiaticus)*, RIGHT AND BELOW
This large spectacular bird usually occurs singly or in pairs and is sparsely distributed across northern Australia. It is able to catch quite large fish, as well as frogs and crustaceans, with its long ebony bill.

White-bellied Sea-Eagle *(Haliaeetus leucogaster)*, ABOVE AND OPPOSITE
A large unmistakable eagle which occurs in coastal regions as well as major wetlands and rivers.
The huge nest is built in a tree or on a coastal cliff and is added to each year. Although it spends
long periods perched on a high vantage point, it may also be seen frequently soaring majestically.

Purple Swamphen *(Porphyrio porphyrio),* ABOVE
A gregarious species which is frequently observed grazing on the grassy margins of ornamental lakes and ponds. Communal breeding is usual, with a single female mating with several males.

Musk Duck *(Biziura lobata),* TOP
This bizarre, dark-coloured duck is very clumsy on land. The remarkable courtship display of the male involves swimming slowly with the tail erect and pouch inflated, while vigorously kicking and whistling.

Plumed Whistling-Duck *(Dendrocygna eytoni)* **and Magpie Goose** *(Anseranas semipalmata),* LEFT
Tropical wetlands are particularly rich and productive, supporting a wide range of waterfowl, frequently in large flocks.

Pied Heron *(Ardea picata),* ABOVE LEFT

A small attractive heron which is confined to tropical regions of northern Australia where it frequently scavenges at sewage farms, garbage tips and campgrounds where it may become tame. It will breed during the wet season, often in large colonies in trees, with other heron species.

White-faced Heron *(Ardea novaehollandiae),* ABOVE RIGHT

One of our most familiar birds, this species is found throughout Australia, usually near water, but at times may be seen feeding in paddocks or on lawns. The loose, untidy nest is built of twigs and placed in a tree, sometimes far from water in small loose colonies.

Nankeen Night Heron *(Nycticorax caledonicus),* ABOVE
Although widespread, this handsome heron is rarely seen due to its nocturnal habits, roosting by day in trees and flying out to feed at night. Juvenile birds have heavily streaked underparts and are frequently confused with bitterns. Pairs usually nest in large colonies.

Black Swan *(Cygnus atratus)*, ABOVE AND OPPOSITE
An elegant bird which is endemic to Australia where it frequently occurs in large flocks. The huge untidy nest of reeds and grass is often built in shallow water. Pairs mate for life and time their breeding according to rainfall to ensure suffient new grass to feed the cygnets.

Coasts & Islands

Australia's coastal habitats are home to a great diversity of birds, many of which are specialists and therefore highly dependent upon these valuable ecosystems. This junction between the land and the sea is extremely productive, being constantly fed by nutrients washed from the land by rivers and swept in from the oceans. The coastal zone comprises a great mix of landforms and habitats and each habitat type provides a unique set of conditions suitable for all of the particular bird community.

Throughout the tropics, muddy mangrove forests and coastal swamps provide refuge for large concentrations of migratory waders such as Grey-tailed Tattlers, Terek Sandpipers and Great Knots.

The steep rocky cliffs and islands which dot the southern coasts provide huge colonies of Australasian Gannets and Shy Albatrosses with nest sites that are safe from predators. Countless thousands of Short-tailed Shearwaters breed in burrows on these turf-covered islands while after dark groups of Little Penguins clamber ashore to feed their waiting chicks.

Sweeping sandy beaches are much loved by humans and also provide the perfect breeding and roosting conditions for several species of terns including Fairy Terns, Little Terns and Crested Terns as well as Silver and Pacific Gulls.

Coral reefs such as the Great Barrier Reef, with its large number of small cays and islands, are havens for numerous varieties of seabirds including the Black Noddies, Brown Boobies, Bridled Terns and Red-tailed Tropicbirds.

Lady Elliot Island lies in the Capricorn Group east of Bundaberg at the southern end of the Great Barrier Reef. This small coral cay (it is possible to walk around the perimeter of the island in 40 minutes) has become in recent years one of the richest islands on the whole of the reef for seabirds. During spring and summer months this island of dazzling white coral is home to huge numbers of nesting birds. When landing by plane on the small grass airstrip, clouds of Crested Terns rise into the air to greet the visitor, before settling back to their eggs and chicks. Tens of thousands of Black Noddies build their fragile nests in the branches of the Casuarina and Pisonia trees which cover much of the island while Common Noddies nest on the ground behind the beaches. Large groups of noddies are frequently seen sunning themselves, each with one outstretched wing, on the lawns of the small resort.

One of the special birds found on Lady Elliot Island is the Red-tailed Tropicbird. This spectacular, large white seabird has a distinctive and extremely long pair of red tail plumes and is frequently seen performing aerial displays over the breeding area, at times including bouts of backward flying. Five or six pairs of these highly vocal seabirds nest under low bushes right in front of the holiday units allowing visitors close-up views of the breeding behaviour of these dramatic birds during spring and early summer.

Great and Least Frigatebirds are often seen floating in the skies over Lady Elliot Island although they do not breed there. These feathered pirates of the ocean are incredibly graceful and accomplished in flight, with a wingspan approaching two metres. They frequently harass noddies, terns and boobies into dropping their catch and also swoop into colonies to snatch unprotected eggs or chicks.

Unfortunately, the loss and degradation of coastal habitats is widespread due to overuse by humans for recreation, housing and industrial development. The full and strict protection of a network of coastal reserves is therefore vital if future generations are to enjoy and marvel at this great diversity of coastal birds.

ABOVE: *The Australasian Gannet breeds on offshore islands.* OPPOSITE: *The Red-tailed Tropicbird has a highly distinctve flight silhouette.*

Pacific Gull *(Larus pacificus),* ABOVE
This endemic species has the largest bill of any of the world's gulls. It is restricted to the coasts and islands of southern Australia and Tasmania where it breeds in loose colonies, usually on offshore islands. The black tail band distinguishes the species from the similar Kelp Gull.

Pied Cormorant *(Phalacrocorax varius),* OPPOSITE
A large cormorant with distinctive black thighs, which is also numerous on inland wetlands and particularly those of the Murray-Darling system. This group of recently fledged juveniles was photographed on an island off the coast of Western Australia.

Little Pied Cormorant *(Phalacrocorax melanoleucos)*, ABOVE
Common throughout much of the continent, this small attractive cormorant is equally at home on small dams and lakes in city parks and on larger waters such as estuaries. The plumage soon becomes waterlogged and then requires hanging out to dry as seen in this picture.

Australian Pelican *(Pelecanus conspicillatus)*, OPPOSITE
Unusually, these nomadic and spectacular birds frequently fish together in groups. Several birds swim together and drive fish into shallow water where they scoop up the fish by simultaneously submerging their heads and huge bills. Breeding colonies may contain up to 1000 pairs.

Osprey *(Pandion haliaetus)*, ABOVE AND LEFT
This bird of prey feeds almost exclusively on fish, which are caught
by diving feet first into the water. The fish are manipulated in the
talons and carried head first to minimise wind resistance.

Shy Albatross *(Diomedea cauta)*, PREVIOUS PAGES
The only albatross to breed within Australian waters is the Shy
Albatross which often scavenges from fishing boats. This colony,
on Albatross Island in Bass Strait, was decimated by harvesting at
the turn of the century, but is now thriving following protection.

White-bellied Sea-Eagle *(Haliaeetus leucogaster),* ABOVE AND OPPOSITE
This large and dramatic eagle is nesting at a height of over 30 metres in a eucalypt tree. The chick seen
at right is approximately three weeks old. The same chick, seen above at 10 weeks, is preparing to
leave the nest by vigorously exercising its growing wings.

Peregrine Falcon *(Falco peregrinus)*
The Peregrine, which preys mostly on birds, is reputed to be the fastest bird on earth. The female falcon (shown on these pages) is larger and more muscular than the male.

White Tern *(Gygis alba),* ABOVE AND OPPOSITE
A single egg is laid, usually balanced on a tree branch, but sometimes on a fern frond or even on
a wooden sign. The chick remains perched on the branch until fledging at 60–70 days. Within the
Australian region, this snow-white tern only breeds on Lord Howe and Norfolk islands.

Black-naped Tern (*Sterna sumatrana*), ABOVE

A tropical tern occurring on cays and islands of northeast Australia. It is usually seen in small groups but readily associates with other tern species at breeding colonies and high tide roosts. Feeding is mostly by plunge-diving for small fish in shallow lagoons.

Little Tern (*Sterna albifrons*), OPPOSITE

An exclusively coastal species which is declining in numbers due to human disturbance at its breeding sites. Positive management in some states by wardening, fencing, provision of artificial islands and controlling access by people has allowed some local increase in numbers.

Crested Tern *(Sterna bergii)*, ABOVE AND RIGHT
The most common Australian tern can be found along the entire
coastline. It breeds on offshore islands in densely packed colonies.
One egg is laid and the chick fledges after about 38 days. During
good seasons, two broods may be raised in succession.

Australasian Gannet (*Morus serrator*), ABOVE AND LEFT
Exclusively marine, it sometimes forages close to shore, particularly
during stormy weather. Australia's only mainland colony has been
established recently on Cape Portland, Victoria due to the provision
of predator-proof, electrified fencing.

Masked Booby *(Sula dactylatra),*
LEFT AND OPPOSITE
Boobies replace gannets in tropical seas and this species breeds on several of Australia's offshore islands, including Cocos (Keeling), Raine and Lord Howe. Small loose colonies are found on grassy slopes above the sea and chicks fledge at about 120 days.

Brown Booby *(Sula leucogaster),* BELOW
Common throughout tropical oceans, the Brown Booby is easily recognised by the deep brown upperparts. This species is often seen roosting on piers, marker buoys, jetties and even boat rigging in harbours. Only one chick is usually raised.

Sooty Oystercatcher *(Haematopus fuliginosus)*, ABOVE
An exclusively coastal species which prefers rocky shores and islands compared to the similar Pied Oystercatcher which prefers sandy beaches or mudflats. Two, sometimes three, eggs are laid in a small depression among rocks.

Mixed flock of Grey-tailed Tattlers *(Tringa brevipes)* ***and Bar-tailed Godwits*** *(Limosa lapponica)*, LEFT
Vast flocks of waders migrate from their breeding grounds in the northern hemisphere to spend the southern summer in Australia. One of the finest sites to view them is the shores of Roebuck Bay, Broome.

Cape Barren Goose (*Cereopsis novaehollandiae*), ABOVE AND RIGHT
This unusual goose has affinities with both shelducks and true geese.
Its stronghold is on the Bass Strait islands, especially small offshore
ones near Flinders Island. It is very territorial.

Buff-banded Rail *(Gallirallus philippensis)*,
OPPOSITE
Although rarely seen on the mainland this colourful
rail has become quite common on many offshore
islands. On islands along the Great Barrier Reef,
such as Lady Elliot, it frequently scavenges for
scraps around campsites and resorts.

Great Frigatebird *(Fregata minor)*, RIGHT
An uncommon visitor to tropical seas of northern
Australia, this large dramatic seabird does, however,
breed on a few islands on the northern Great Barrier
Reef. It frequently harasses other seabirds to steal
any fish they have caught.

Silvereye *(Zosterops lateralis)*, BELOW
Although this small greenish bird is common
across much of east and southeast Australia, this
subspecies is restricted to islands of the Capricorn
and Bunker groups of the Great Barrier Reef.

Common Noddy *(Anous stolidus)*, ABOVE
This strongly gregarious species breeds commonly on various tropical islands including Lady Elliot and Lord Howe. The larger colonies will often include Sooty Terns. Their nest is usually made of leaves and is placed in a bush on the ground.

Little Penguins *(Eudyptula minor)*, OPPOSITE
This smallest of the world's penguins will usually mate for life and will sometimes breed in large colonies. They make their nest in a burrow among sand dunes or sometimes between rocks and two eggs are incubated for up to 36 days.

Forests

From its perch at the top of a verdant tree fern the Superb Lyrebird poured forth its song. Intricate and melodious, the full-throated song carried a full kilometre across the forested and misty valley. At times the male Superb Lyrebird would break into bouts of mimicry—first a Yellow-tailed Black-Cockatoo, then the cackle of a Kookaburra, then the fluted whistle of a Grey Shrike-Thrush followed by the crack of an Eastern Whipbird, while all the time holding the shimmering curtain of tail streamers and lyres over his back and head. After a few minutes the lyrebird hopped to the ground and raced through the undergrowth to a mound of earth which had been raked clear of vegetation and once more the loud and penetrating song echoed across the valley.

Close by an Eastern Yellow Robin was clinging to a small bush stem before flitting to the edge of the mound to snatch an insect, while from overhead came the excited calls of a small flock of Crimson Rosellas winging their way into the forested unknown.

The densest cover of vegetation occurs in forests and there are several types found within Australia. Rainforests, both tropical and temperate, are found right along the eastern seaboard and in Tasmania. Rainforests are composed of trees with soft and delicate foliage compared to sclerophyll forests which are dominated by eucalypts with hard and leathery foliage. Each type of forest has its own distinct group of birds, many of which are forest specialists and therefore unable to live anywhere else.

Approximately 140 species of birds occur in the rainforest, including over 60 species only found within this habitat. Many of these birds such as Southern Cassowaries, fig-parrots and bowerbirds are fruit eaters and the passing of seeds unharmed through their digestive system aids in the dispersal of rainforest plants.

Although the heaviest of all Australian birds, the Southern Cassowary is difficult to spot in the dim light of a tropical rainforest. These huge, spectacular birds are highly specialised with a striking horn or casque on the top of the head which helps protect the bird as it moves through the tangled forest. Cassowaries have strong stout legs and huge feet which are used for fighting when the cassowary leaps into the air and strikes out with its strong claws. The Southern Cassowary, as well as the closely related Emu, is a member of the ratite family, all of which are flightless, with hair-like feathers and three large forward-pointing toes.

Bowerbirds, which are closely related to Birds of Paradise, are restricted to New Guinea and Australia, and all species are well known for their unique behaviour of building elaborate twin columns of sticks covered with a variety of decorations. The largest species of bowerbird is the Great Bowerbird which is found throughout the forests and woodlands of tropical Australia. Males build quite elaborate and thick bowers which are concealed under a bush or other low foliage. Bowers are tended by a single male throughout the year and the walls are always aligned on a north-south axis. The display areas at each end of the bower are profusely decorated with white objects such as snail shells, bones and pieces of light coloured glass. One bower I was photographing recently near Katherine Gorge held numerous metal washers, roofing screws and several 20 cent pieces! Great Bowerbirds are somewhat sombre in colour with a hidden mauve crest on the back of the head which is raised during display.

Although rainforests cover only a tiny proportion (about 0.3 per cent) of Australia's land surface this incredibly diverse habitat extends to nearly two million hectares, much of which is protected by National Park or World Heritage designation.

ABOVE: *The Tasmanian Masked Owl is the world's largest barn owl.*
OPPOSITE: *The Crimson Rosella is common in eastern forests.*

Green Rosella *(Platycercus caledonicus)*, ABOVE
Found only in Tasmania and on Bass Strait islands, this mainly green
and yellow parrot is common in most wooded habitats. During the
winter, large flocks of up to 80 birds may be seen.

Crimson Rosella *(Platycercus elegans)*
and Australian King Parrot *(Alisterus scapularis)*, RIGHT
Both species are common in the forests of eastern Australia. They
frequently visit gardens, parks or campgrounds, often in flocks to
feed on fruit or seed put out to attract them.

Australian King Parrot *(Alisterus scapularis)*, ABOVE AND LEFT
This quite distinctive parrot is visible at camp grounds and picnic
areas in national parks. The male (seen at left) is distinguished by
its bright colours whereas the female (above) is much duller. Highly
vocal and wary of predators, it feeds in foliage on seeds and nuts.

Scaly-breasted Lorikeet *(Trichoglossus chlorolepidotus),* ABOVE LEFT
The only lorikeet with a completely green head, it feeds on nectar, fruit, pollen, insects and seeds.
Endemic to Australia, it is common in some eastern coastal districts where it often associates
with Rainbow Lorikeets in large and noisy flocks.

Red-collared Lorikeet *(Trichoglossus rubritorquis),* ABOVE RIGHT
One of the commonest parrots of the Top End and frequently seen in Darwin. These birds are
often very approachable, especially when feeding on the many paperbark and eucalyptus blossoms
in parks and gardens. The screeching active flocks also visit garden feeders.

Regent Parrot *(Polytelis anthopeplus),* ABOVE
An attractive, slender, long-tailed parrot which occurs in two distinct populations, both of which
have declined in numbers. It particularly favours Mallee areas for foraging and feeds mainly on the
ground on seeds, fruit and blossom. The nest is placed in a tree hollow.

Rainbow Lorikeet *(Trichoglossus haematodus),* ABOVE AND RIGHT
A brightly coloured and abundant species which is widespread in
coastal districts of eastern Australia. Flocks are extremely vocal,
continually screeching while gathering to feed on native blossom.
It has been introduced into Perth, Western Australia.

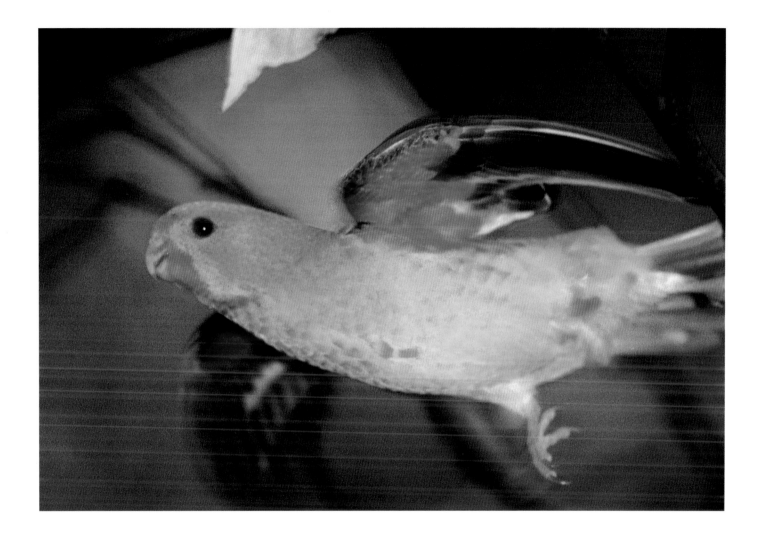

Swift Parrot *(Lathamus discolor)*, ABOVE
This fast-flying parrot only breeds in eastern and northern Tasmania where it appears to be decreasing. The blossom from Blue Gums provides the major source of food during the breeding season although the diet is sometimes supplemented with insects and their larvae.

Orange-bellied Parrot *(Neophema chrysogaster)*, OPPOSITE
Possibly Australia's rarest bird, this diminutive parrot breeds in forests of southwest Tasmania where it feeds on the seeds of herbs and grasses. Recovery is being hampered by destruction of their winter habitat on the mainland coast and lack of burning of the Button Grass plains in Tasmania.

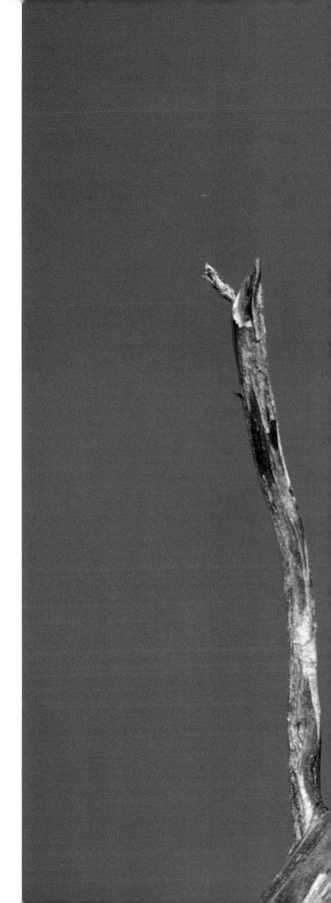

Red-tailed Black-Cockatoo *(Calyptorhynchus banksii),*
ABOVE AND RIGHT
This large spectacular cockatoo is widespread across much of
mainland Australia. Large, conspicuous, noisy flocks may still
be seen, particularly in the Top End and north of Perth, Western
Australia, where they feed on fruit, seeds and bulbs.

Tasmanian Masked Owl *(Tyto novaehollandiae),* ABOVE
A large secretive bird which is completely nocturnal and larger than
the mainland race. Females are considerably larger than males and
are able to prey on bandicoots and possums.

Blue-winged Kookaburra *(Dacelo leachii),* LEFT
Similar in habits to the Laughing Kookaburra, this unusual bird is
common in the wetter forests of the tropics. It feeds mainly on
ground-dwelling insects, especially grasshoppers.

Australian Brush-Turkey *(Alectura lathami)*, ABOVE
One of three Australian megapodes (mound builders) it remains common in coastal rainforests
of Queensland and northern coastal New South Wales. It rapidly becomes tame near picnic sites
and camp grounds and may even be encountered in gardens of suburban Brisbane.

Southern Cassowary *(Casuarius casuarius)*, OPPOSITE
Solitary and elusive, the Southern Cassowary is Australia's heaviest bird. It inhabits pockets of
rainforest at all altitudes in northwest Queensland but numbers are declining due to the clearing
of its rainforest habitat. Many cassowaries are also killed on roads.

Regent Bowerbird *(Sericulus chrysocephalus)*, ABOVE
This brilliantly coloured bowerbird lives in eastern rainforests where
it builds a bower in dense cover. Ornaments such as berries, snail
shells and leaves are arranged between the walls of the bower.

Satin Bowerbird *(Ptilonorhynchus violaceus)*, RIGHT
A common bowerbird in eastern coastal forests which builds a neat
bower of sticks. A large range of mainly blue ornaments are placed
in front of the bower but some yellow objects are also used.

Superb Lyrebird *(Menura novaehollandiae),* ABOVE AND LEFT
This splendid bird inhabits the dense wet forests of the southeast
mainland and Tasmania where it has been introduced. It usually
breeds during winter and the bulky domed nest is built close to
ground level, sometimes against a tree fern, bank or tree stump.

Woodlands & Plains

Large tracts of the Australian continent are covered by woodlands merging through scrub into open plains. The woodlands are dominated by eucalypts but there are acacias or even tea trees. These woodlands include the mallee which once covered much of south-east Australia, mulga which is acacia-dominated and generally found further north, and brigalow which covers huge areas of outback Queensland.

There are many bird species that range across several of these habitat types, including the Emu, Laughing Kookaburra, Bush Stone-Curlew, Wedge-tailed Eagle, Barn Owl and Major Mitchell's Cockatoo.

The large, flightless Emu is widespread across Australia and is equally at home in woodlands, dense scrub or open plains. These nomadic birds are able to travel large distances in search of water or fresh green vegetation, rapidly leaving areas suffering from drought.

Bush Stone-Curlews are usually located by their eerie nocturnal wailings. Due to their secretive habits, Bush Stone-Curlews are rarely seen and roost by day on the ground, frequently under trees or shrubs. When disturbed, they prefer to crouch and freeze or slowly stalk off rather than take flight. Unfortunately these intriguing birds have become rare in many southern regions due to predation and the destruction of habitat.

In contrast, that popular chortling comic, the Laughing Kookaburra, remains common and widespread over much of eastern and southwestern Australia where it has been introduced. Laughing Kookaburras are able to survive without open water and have a wide ranging diet which includes insects, snakes, lizards, small mammals and the occasional small bird.

Woodlands interspersed with open plains provide the perfect conditions for many species of raptor including the large and spectacular Wedge-tailed Eagle (Australia's largest bird of prey), Australian Hobby, Brown Falcon, Nankeen Kestrel and the rare, beautiful Black-breasted Buzzard. This bird is sparsely distributed across much of inland and northern Australia and is frequently seen while driving north from Alice Springs to Tennant Creek. The well known ornithologist Gould referred to this bird's amazing habit of driving Emus from their nests and breaking their eggs by dropping stones on them. He heard this account from Aboriginal people and it has only recently been substantiated by biologists.

The Australian Hobby is a dapper small falcon resembling a miniature Peregrine Falcon and preys mainly on insects and small birds which it hunts on the wing with an aggressive and dashing flight, often at night. Hobbies are widespread in Australia, although somewhat secretive. Like all falcons, breeding pairs occupy abandoned nests of birds such as ravens and they defend them fiercely during the nesting season.

Australia is home to several species of unusual birds which build nests of mud, such as Apostlebirds and White-winged Choughs. They live in social clans of up to 20 individuals although in winter, foraging flocks of over 50 birds may be seen. Apostlebirds, named because flocks of 12 were considered usual, are sedentary and occupy permanent feeding territories of about 10 to 20 hectares in inland eastern and northern Australia. These strongly communal birds share in most aspects of their behaviour including building the mud nest on a horizontal branch of a tree. Eggs are laid by several females and incubation and the feeding of chicks is also shared by several of these fascinating birds. The nesting territory is vigorously defended by members of the clan.

All life is therefore intertwined and interdependent and birds are entirely dependent upon these diverse ecosystems. Our rich diversity of birdlife along with their habitats are critical components of the environment, and it is vital that they are managed wisely.

ABOVE: *The Laughing Kookaburra is the largest kingfisher.* OPPOSITE: *A male Emu guards its clutch of pale blue eggs.*

Emu *(Dromaius novaehollandiae)*, ABOVE AND RIGHT
Remaining abundant in many regions, the omnivorous Emu has
probably benefited from European settlement because of the
provision of dams and waterholes. Incubation (about 60 days)
and chick rearing is carried out entirely by the male.

Little Corella *(Cacatua sanguinea)*, FOLLOWING PAGES
Widespread and abundant on mainland Australia, this nomadic bird
often occurs in huge flocks which forage for bulbs and seeds mainly
on the ground. Flocks are particularly active and raucous before
going to roost in trees often near waterholes.

Malleefowl *(Leipoa ocellata),* ABOVE
This wary and elusive bird inhabits the semi-arid regions of southeast Australia where numbers
are decreasing due to land clearance and predation by foxes. The diet includes flowers and shoots
of herbs, which are destroyed by rabbits and sheep, and large quantities of insects.

Apostlebird *(Struthidea cinerea),* ABOVE LEFT
These territorial birds live in close-knit communities of about 8 to 20 birds which spend most of their lives on the ground. They are opportunistic feeders eating large quantities of insects in the summer and seeds during the winter. They need to drink frequently, particularly during summer.

Great Bowerbird *(Chlamydera nuchalis),* ABOVE RIGHT
Males construct new bowers, usually hidden under a bush, each year. Only found in the tropical north, these birds feed largely on fruit. Males are fastidious in keeping the bower walls free of leaves and the cleared area in front of the bower is decorated with shells and small pebbles.

Galah (*Cacatua roseicapilla*), ABOVE
Since European settlement, Galahs have increased their range
dramatically and flocks of these colourful birds are now a feature
of urban centres as well as the outback.

Common Bronzewing (*Phaps chalcoptera*), LEFT
A common bird found in open woodlands which is easily confused
with the similar Brush Bronzewing. It forages on the ground beneath
wattles, eucalypts and on grassland edges on a variety of seeds.

Red-winged Parrot (*Aprosmictus erythropterus*), ABOVE
A generally wary and nomadic bird which spends most of its time feeding on blossom, seeds, pollen and nectar in the foliage of trees. The flight is distinctive, with strong but erratic and deeply undulating wing beats, only rarely descending to the ground to drink.

Mallee Ringneck *(Barnardius barnardi),* ABOVE
Now generally regarded as a race of the Australian Ringneck, this familiar species remains common across much of the south central mainland. The breeding season varies depending on conditions and 4 to 6 eggs are incubated in a tree hollow.

Sulphur-crested Cockatoo *(Cacatua galerita),* ABOVE LEFT AND OPPOSITE
Flocks of these loud raucous cockatoos are very much a feature across northern and eastern Australia.
A familiar cage bird, it is expanding its range, particularly within urban centres. The varied diet
consists of seeds, fruit, nuts, bulbs, insects and their larvae.

Major Mitchell's Cockatoo *(Cacatua leadbeateri),* ABOVE RIGHT
One of our most beautiful parrots, it has unfortunately decreased in many areas due to the clearing of
native vegetation and trapping for aviculture. It favours semi-arid habitats such as mallee, mulga and
native pine woodland. It is often seen feeding on the fruit of wild melons.

Brown falcon *(Falco berigora)*, ABOVE AND RIGHT
One of Australia's most numerous and widespread birds of prey,
the Brown falcon can occur in a variety of colour forms. The
three chicks huddled together at right are just about to fledge
from their home in a disused nest.

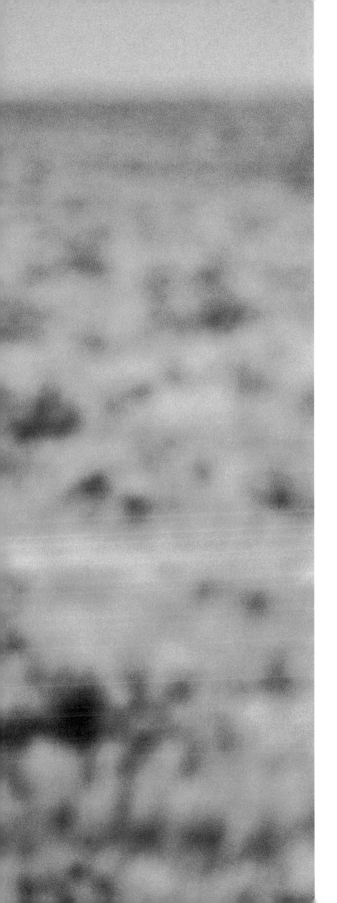

Black-breasted Buzzard *(Hamirostra melanosternon)*, ABOVE
Behaving in a way only recently confirmed by biologists, the buzzard
seen here is attempting to break an Emu egg with a stone. Several
attempts were made with different stones before the buzzard was
able to break the egg and drink the contents.

Nankeen Kestrel *(Falco cenchroides)*, LEFT
One of Australia's most widespread and abundant birds of prey is
seen here nesting in a disused ravens' nest on the Nullarbor Plain.
The female has just returned and is about to feed the four rapidly
growing chicks with prey captured by the male.

Australian Hobby *(Falco longipennis)*, ABOVE AND RIGHT
This small falcon preys chiefly on insects and small birds which
are hunted with a fierce and dashing flight. Breeding territories
are fiercely defended against intruders and eggs are usually laid
in disused ravens' nests high in a tree.

Tawny Frogmouth *(Podargus strigoides)*, ABOVE LEFT AND RIGHT
A well known bird of the night which is usually spotted in the headlights of a car. Trees are required for daytime roosting and pairs occupy permanent territories. It feeds on invertebrates as well as frogs and small mammals. The bird pictured above left is a rare albino.

Barn Owl *(Tyto alba)*, OPPOSITE
This cosmopolitan species is widespread across Australia although it requires open country to hunt over. House Mice comprise the bulk of prey items and owl numbers increase to take advantage of mice plagues. Tree hollows are favoured for nesting although old buildings are also used.

Blue-faced Honeyeater *(Entomyzon cyanotis)*, ABOVE
One of Australia's largest and most striking honeyeaters which is
common over eastern and northern regions. Up to 30 of these
arboreal birds often form noisy flocks.

Red Wattlebird *(Anthochaera carunculata)*, RIGHT
A locally nomadic or migratory species found in southeast
Australia. It inhabits woodland, parks and gardens feeding on
fruit, nectar, manna and insects including caterpillars.

Beautiful Firetail *(Emblema bellum)*, OPPOSITE
This attractive small finch is found in coastal south-east Australia and in Tasmania where it is most common. Courtship behaviour involves the carrying of a long grass strip and a bulky domed nest is built.

Superb Fairy-Wren *(Malurus cyaneus)*, RIGHT
This highly social species lives in family groups that maintain their own territory. A familiar garden bird, it has expanded its range since European settlement. The bird depicted here is a male.

Superb Fairy-Wren *(Malurus cyaneus)*, BELOW
Co-operative groups of this species consist of non-breeding birds of both sexes, first year birds, one mature female and a dominant male. An adult female is pictured below.

Willie Wagtail (*Rhipidura leucophrys*), OPPOSITE
Found throughout mainland Australia, this common species frequently becomes confiding or tame. The adult seen here is covering the chicks during extreme temperatures of 46 degrees Celsius at Broome Bird Observatory, Western Australia.

Dusky Robin (*Melanodryas vittata*), ABOVE LEFT
Endemic to Tasmania, where it is widespread and common, it also occurs on King and Flinders islands. It hunts by perching motionless on a low branch or stump before dropping down to grab an insect.

Eastern Yellow Robin (*Eopsaltria australis*), LEFT
The typical hunting posture of this attractive and common species is to cling to the sides of a sapling. The exquisite nest is a small cup of bark strips bound with cobwebs and placed in a small tree.

Striated Pardalote *(Pardalotus striatus)*, ABOVE
A nomadic and sociable bird, except while breeding, it feeds mainly in tree foliage. It may be located
by its distinctive and persistent two syllable 'chip chip' call, uttered during spring. The nest is either
placed in a tree hollow or a tunnel in a bank.

Spotted Pardalote *(Pardalotus punctatus),* ABOVE
A tiny jewel-like bird, distinguished from other pardalotes by its bright red rump, yellow throat and clear white spots. The domed nest of bark strips is placed at the end of a tunnel in a bank. Unlike the previous species which is migratory, the Spotted Pardalote is sedentary and solitary in most areas.

The Arid Centre

One recent spring dawn, I gazed across a wide expanse of deep red dunefields on the border of the Simpson Desert, central Australia. The winter rains had been exceptional and water was flowing along a normally dry and rocky river bed. Close by a pair of White-browed Woodswallows were busy building their nest in a stunted eucalypt. From above drifted the excited musical chattering of a small flock of Budgerigars as they hurried to a nearby clump of trees to prospect the many nesting hollows.

As I slowly walked through a carpet of wildflowers, a brief flash of crimson exploded from beneath my feet. I carefully parted the flowers to reveal the nest of a Crimson Chat with three rapidly growing chicks. During the next two hours of patient searching, I found another six nests of Crimson Chat, most with eggs. Frequently the female would attempt to lead me away from the nest with a fluttering broken wing display. All of the nests were built close to ground level in low vegetation or among fallen dead branches.

The land was alive. The winter rains had sparked an explosion of vegetation growth in a normally arid landscape. The desert was in bloom and the resulting profusion of flowering plants gave rise to an explosion in the population of insects. This event, in turn, triggered the breeding behaviour of insectivorous birds such as Crimson Chats and White-browed Woodswallows. The Budgerigars and Zebra Finches, both seed-eating birds, had timed their breeding cycle perfectly. Now there was a multitude of flowering plants and grasses in seed so that the parrot and finch chicks could be raised on this bountiful harvest.

Vast areas of central Australia are covered by arid scrublands or grasslands which at times can be densely populated with a variety of birds. These birds are usually nomadic and are able to move rapidly to areas which have been transformed by good rains. I recently counted about 50 active nests of Zebra Finches in one small tree. Incredibly, at the same time a Brown Falcon was sitting on four eggs in a disused ravens' nest in the top of the same tree!

Some of the birds which respond to the favourable conditions that occur after rain in arid lands include Cockatiels, Mulga Parrots, Princess Parrots and Pied and Black Honeyeaters.

Although commonly kept as a cage bird in most parts of the world, the Budgerigar, the only member of its genus, is confined to mainland Australia, principally the arid interior. They are most active during early morning when sometimes large flocks may be seen visiting waterholes to drink.

During a recent visit to central Australia, Budgerigars were very conspicuous, and I often encountered small flocks crossing roads, with large numbers breeding in eucalypts along seasonal watercourses or in stands of mulga. Some small trees held 10 or more pairs of these delightful small parrots and the air was filled with their excited warblings and chatterings.

The attractive Spinifex Pigeon has become adapted to living permanently in the arid spinifex-covered grasslands and hills of central Australia. Being dependent on access to water, these small, long-crested pigeons congregate close to waterholes during drought, breeding only after rain. Like bronzewing pigeons, male Spinifex Pigeons engage in a bowing display which sometimes involves bouts of aggression.

True deserts hold little life, but the semi-arid or arid regions of Australia (often referred to as deserts) are ecologically rich and frequently covered by thick scrub, low trees and grasses. It is important to manage these vulnerable areas sympathetically if we are to conserve the rich assemblage of birds which depend upon them.

ABOVE: *A pair of White-browed Woodswallows courting.*
OPPOSITE: *A Wedge-tailed Eagle alights on a large boulder.*

Wedge-tailed Eagle *(Aquila audax)*, ABOVE AND RIGHT
A large raptor, affectionately known as a 'Wedgie'. In recent years
rabbits have become a staple food although road-killed kangaroos
are also popular. As eagles age they become progressively darker
until they are almost black as seen above.

Zebra Finch *(Taeniopygia guttata),* ABOVE
A social and abundant bird which breeds in loose colonies, usually near water. Communal nests are also built for roosting and it feeds mainly on the ground on grass seeds, grass-shoot tips and insects. Young birds are able to breed at about 90 days when they attain adult plumage.

Cockatiel *(Nymphicus hollandicus),* OPPOSITE
A migratory species whose movements are influenced primarily by rainfall. Cockatiels appear to have increased their population since European settlement due to the provision of permanent watering points for stock. This popular cage bird feeds on seeds of native shrubs, trees and grasses.

Budgerigar *(Melopsittacus undulatus)*, ABOVE AND OPPOSITE
A highly gregarious species which sometimes occurs in huge flocks of thousands. During courtship, while pairs are prospecting for nest sites, these delightful birds will often allow a close approach, making photography quite easy. Adult males are recognised by the blue above their beaks.

Princess Parrot *(Polytelis alexandrae),* ABOVE
One of Australia's most beautiful and elusive parrots, it is confined to the central western interior.
It is highly nomadic and breeding has only rarely been recorded. The Princess Parrot forages mainly
on the ground on the seeds of acacias, spinifex and herbs.

Rainbow Bee-Eater *(Merops ornatus),* ABOVE LEFT

A summer migrant to Australia which is entirely dependent upon insects for food. It frequently nests colonially, tunnelling into sandy soil and laying 4 to 5 white eggs. Incubation and the raising of chicks is carried out by several individuals.

Red-backed Kingfisher *(Todirhamphus pyrrhopygia),* ABOVE RIGHT

Often found far from water but always close to trees, this endemic kingfisher often perches on overhead wires and feeds on insects, reptiles and frogs. The nest is placed in a tunnel in a bank or termite mound. A mournful, harsh alarm call is often heard near the nest.

Australian Bustard *(Ardeotis kori)*, OPPOSITE
A large omnivorous bird which has decreased in numbers, particularly in southern regions due to hunting and predation by foxes. Bustards are able to survive long periods without drinking and breed following periods of rainfall.

Crimson Chat *(Epthianura tricolor)*,
TOP AND BOTTOM LEFT
This striking bird is quite gregarious and nomadic. The adult male, pictured here, is unmistakable during the breeding season. It inhabits open inland areas, particularly near salt lakes, and breeds in loose colonies in low vegetation.

Spinifex Pigeon *(Geophaps plumifera)*,
FOLLOWING PAGE
A colourful small pigeon which inhabits areas of spinifex and acacia scrub across north-west and central Australia where there is permanent water. This ground-nesting pigeon lives mostly in small groups and rarely flies except when hard pressed.

White-browed Woodswallows *(Artamus superciliosus)*, PAGE 127
A pair of White-browed Woodswallows.

Index